DATE DUE

The Making of a Champion

An International Soccer Star

Heinemann Library

Chicago, Illinois

Ben Godsal

Customer Service 888-454-2279

Visit our website at www.heinemannlibrary.com

Designed by Heinemann Library.
Printed in China by WKT Company Limited.

09 08 07 06 05
10 9 8 7 6 5 4 3 2 1

Library of Congress Cataloging-in-Publication Data

Godsal, Ben, 1976-
  An International Soccer Star / Ben Godsal.
    p. cm. -- (The making of a champion)
  Includes bibliographical references and index.
  ISBN 1-4034-5365-9 (lib. bdg.) -- ISBN 1-4034-5549-X (pbk.)
  1. Soccer--Juvenile literature. 2. Soccer players--Juvenile literature. I. Title. II. Series.
  GV943.25.G56 2004
  796.334--dc22
                              2004003874

Acknowledgements
The publishers would like to thank the following for permission to reproduce photographs:

Empics pp. **5 top**, **5 bottom**, 6, 8, 9, 20, **21 top**, **21 bottom**, 22 (Mike Egerton), 26, **27 bottom**, 28, 29, 30, **31 top**, **31 bottom**, 32, 33, 34 (Tony Marshall), 35, 38, 39, 40, **41 bottom**; Getty Images pp. 4 (Clive Brunskill), **7 top**, **7 bottom** (SMG), 10 (Hamish Blair), 11 (Alex Livesey), 12 (Firo Foto), **13 top** (Shaun Botterill), **13 bottom** (Grazia Neri), 14, 15 (Shaun Botterill), 16 (Gary M. Prior), 17 (Phil Cole), **19 top** (Mike Hewitt), **19 bottom** (Alex Livesey), 23 (Liu Jin), 24 (Ben Radford), 25 (Stu Forester), **27 top** (Doug Pensinger), 36 (Laurence Griffiths), **37 top** (Jeff Gross), **37 bottom** (Shaun Botterill), **41 top** (Jonathan Daniel), 42, 43 (Ben Radford).

Cover photograph reproduced with permission of Philippe Desmazes/AFP/Getty Images.

Every effort has been made to contact copyright holders of any material reproduced in this book. Any omissions will be rectified in subsequent printings if notice is given to the publishers.

The paper used to print this book comes from sustainable resources.

Contents

The global game

Soccer is the most popular sport in the world. It is played by millions of people around the globe—on green fields, tropical beaches, and dusty roads. It is played by the rich and the poor, the young and the old, and by men and women of every color, religion, and background. Soccer brings people together. You can go anywhere in the world—to places where people speak a different language, eat different food, or follow a different religion—but the game remains the same.

The journey

On September 22, 1976, a boy named Ronaldo De Lima was born in a poor neighborhood in Brazil. He was raised by his mother, who was a waitress at a pizza restaurant. Almost as soon as he could walk, Ronaldo spent most of his time playing soccer with his friends. As he got older, this worried his mother, who wanted him to spend more time studying. But it soon became clear Ronaldo had a special talent. When he was thirteen years old, he told his friends, "One day I will become the best in the world." At the age of fifteen, he started playing for a professional team near Rio de Janeiro.

Life and death

Soccer is not as popular in the United States as it is in the rest of the world. Much of the rest of world views soccer as Americans see their favorite baseball, basketball, and football teams. For example, a famous British soccer coach once said, "Some people believe [soccer] is a matter of life and death... I can assure you it's much, much more important than that."

Ronaldo wears the famous Brazilian number nine shirt. He has come a long way since he kicked a ball around the streets of Rio de Janeiro as a child.

Popularity fact

The last World Cup—played in Japan and South Korea in 2002—was watched on TV by nearly 30 billion people around the globe. More people watched the eight-week tournament than watched any other event in history. It was broadcast in 213 countries with each live match averaging a TV audience of around 356 million people. By the time Brazil beat Germany in the championship game, more than a billion homes had tuned in to watch.

Another example of soccer's hold on its fans occurred in Great Britain in 1957. That year a man named Harold Macmillan became the British prime minister, but the local newspaper in his home town did not think his election was important enough for the front page. Instead, the main story was a report about the local soccer team. Imagine if the newspaper in George W. Bush's home town of Midland, Texas, would have put a story on its front page about the Dallas Cowboys the day after his election as president in 2000.

Children in Africa play soccer on a dusty field.

How the game began

Soccer, as the game is played today, has only been around for about 150 years. The modern version was first played by boys at private schools and universities in England. However, a similar sport was played more than 2,000 years before that—in China. The first ever game was said to have been played to mark the Chinese emperor's birthday in 206 B.C.E. Two teams had to kick a ball made of horsehair in between their opponents' posts. Legend has it that the winners were rewarded with a special feast, while the losers had their heads chopped off!

The next stage

Versions of the game continued to be played with the rules changing all the time. However, in the 1860s the English Football Association—soccer is known as football in much of the rest of the world—wrote down an official set of rules. The rules remain much the same today. The first league was formed in 1888 and was made up of twelve teams.

Meanwhile, the first game between two countries was in 1872 when England and Scotland played to 0–0 draw, or tie, in Glasgow, Scotland.

In 1878, England played Scotland in one of the first ever international matches.

The early greats

As the game matured, great players began to emerge from all over the world. There was the English striker Tom Finney who played in the 1950s and the spectacular Brazilian Pelé. There was also Alfredo di Stefano *(right, in white)* who played for one of the most successful teams of all time—Real Madrid of the Spanish league in the 1960s. He was a forward who could pass, dribble, and shoot with great skill.

Spreading the word

It was not long before the game began to catch on around the world. First, it spread to countries in Europe. And then, as more people began to travel, so did soccer. One of the reasons the game is so popular is because it can be played anywhere. It was also one of the ways European travelers kept themselves occupied when they were overseas. There was no television, but they could play soccer—as could anyone who happened to be watching. And so the game spread. By the time the first World Cup kicked off in 1930, soccer was the most popular sport on Earth. However, it was not until more recently—in the 1980s and 1990s—that the game started to become popular in the United States.

Into the modern age

Soccer today is a different game than it was 50 years ago. It is played by athletes who are quicker, faster, and stronger than ever before. Women's soccer is also growing. The soccer stars of today have to work harder than ever if they are to become champions.

English goalie Margaret Turner (second from right) punches the ball away from danger in a match against Scotland in 1966. But women's soccer would not gain popularity until many years later.

Getting started

Great soccer players can pass the ball 30 yards (27.4 meters) to their teammates or trap it with one quick movement of their foot. They can score great goals and make crucial tackles, too. But using these skills repeatedly throughout a soccer season takes a great deal of practice. Getting to the top in soccer takes a mixture of natural talent and hard work. Getting started is the easy part.

You can start your career anywhere. Here, boys from Bolivia are taking their first steps to try to become the soccer stars of the future.

Taking the first step

Most children kick balls around as soon as they can walk. Aside from soccer cleats and shin guards, a ball is the only equipment a player needs. Great players of the past, such as Diego Maradona of Argentina, first learned the game by kicking a ball around the streets of their neighborhood. Uneven road surfaces meant the ball bounced off in funny directions, often making it difficult for the youngsters to control. But all that practice on uneven streets can eventually pay off. As players like Maradona have shown, a soccer star can start their career anywhere and still become a soccer champion.

The referee

One person a professional game always needs is a referee. The referee's job is to control the game. He or she does this by blowing the whistle after a foul. If a player commits a bad foul, the referee will show a yellow card. This is a warning. A second serious foul often means a red card, and the player can be ejected from the game. A player can also receive a red card for committing a single foul that the referee considers to be particularly dangerous.

Camps and junior leagues

Children have many opportunities to get an organized introduction to soccer. Some learn the basics at school. For others, soccer camps are held during holidays where children can develop their skills. There are also leagues in cities and towns all over the country run by the American Youth Soccer Organization (AYSO). Here, children as young as four years old are taught the game by coaches and volunteers. They learn the basics skills of the game and are encouraged to enjoy themselves.

Cleats fact

Soccer cleats have come a long way since the early days. At the beginning of the 1900s, cleats weighed more than a pound and became twice as heavy when it rained. Players were carrying around the equivalent of a bag of sugar on each foot. Now, soccer cleats are big business. Former Australian star Craig Johnston realized that finding the right shape for a soccer shoe would lead to greater ball control. After experimenting, he came up with the Predator boot. The use of light materials and a shaped toe meant more swerve and power for shooting. The boot was made by Adidas and is now one of the most popular around.

Cleats worn by professional players are now the right shape and weight, giving players greater control of the ball.

The art of attack

Being a great attacking, or offensive, player is about more than just scoring goals. Of course, all players love the glory of putting the ball in the back of the net but the best forwards, or strikers, have more to their games than that.

Key qualities

The best forwards all have the following qualities:

- Control—to get the team a scoring opportunity, a player needs to keep the ball close when running and be able to pass accurately to a teammate when the time is right.

- Confidence—strikers need confidence to perform at their best. When a star forward stops scoring goals, it is often because he or she has lost confidence.

- Cunning—good strikers are clever. They will disguise their running patterns or the way they shoot so that the goalkeeper is kept guessing which way the ball will go.

- Team play—most goals are a team effort. Teams usually play with two strikers, and it is important that they know how each other plays. Spain's Real Madrid has two strikers—Raúl and Ronaldo—that have scored many goals together. Ronaldo knows how to create opportunities for his teammates, while Raúl is a penalty-box striker. This means he spends a lot of time inside the penalty box near the goal. The two players complement each other perfectly.

Harry Kewell, a star in England, combines control, cunning, confidence, and teamwork and is one of the top players in his position in the world. He is also very quick and creates as many goals for his teammates as he scores himself.

Raúl González of Real Madrid is one of the best finishers in the game. In other words, when he shoots, he usually hits the target.

Scoring goals

Goals are scored in all sorts of ways, from the simple close range tap-in, to the curling 30-yard (27.4-meter) bomb. Whether the ball comes off the head, the body, or the foot, the end result is the same. However they are scored, goals are what the crowds come to see.

Curling fact

When a player's path to the goal is blocked by an opponent, he or she will often try to curve the ball around the opposing player. The secret behind curving or curling the ball is to hit it off-center, which makes it spin through the air. It is not only forwards who need this skill but free-kick takers, too. They often need to curve the ball around a wall of players in order to hit the target. Curling is a difficult skill that takes hours of practice.

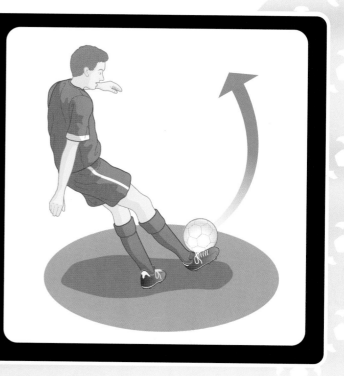

Pulling the strings— the midfielders

Midfielders are like actors—they play many different roles. The best midfielders know how to defend, attack, and do everything in between. They must also be in great shape as they have to cover almost every blade of grass—chasing the ball down when on defense, passing the ball on offense, and supporting the strikers when their team has the ball. Although players like Zinedine Zidane of France can fill all these roles, sometimes teams give separate instructions to each midfielder. This is so that the more creative players can concentrate on offense, while the best defenders can help on defense.

Zinedine Zidane

The French midfielder and 2003 World [Soccer Player] of the Year is thought by many people to be the world's best midfielder. Called Zizou, he helped France win the World Cup in 1998 and then took them to the European Championships two years later. Zidane's French teammate Bixente Lizarazu once said, "When we don't know what to do, we just give the ball to Zizou and he works something out."

Passing the Brazilian way

Perhaps the most important weapon of the midfielder is the ability to pass well. The Brazilian team has a long tradition of passing in soccer. From players such as Zico and Pelé years ago, to modern day wizards such as Rivaldo, Brazilians have always known how to pass the ball. It is the Brazilians ability to put many crisp passes together that often put their strikers in position to score a goal.

Claudio Reyna was one of the success stories of the U.S. World Cup campaign in 2002. He is known for his energy and terrific all-round game.

- All players, especially midfielders, should be able to pass the ball to a player on the opposite side of the field or to play a simple give and go with a teammate just a couple of feet away.

- Putting the right force behind a pass is also important. The ability to drive the ball hard onto a player's path or to send it delicately to a running teammate in stride are signs of passing excellence.

- One of the things that sets the good passers apart from the great ones is the ability to disguise where the ball is going. Doing this can confuse the defense and create a scoring opportunity. England's David Beckham is a master at disguise. He may look like he is going to pass to one player, but by cleverly changing the angle of his foot, he can send it to someone completely different.

France's Patrick Vieira is a midfielder known for his tough defense, but he is a good passer, too.

Solid as a rock— the defenders

While it is the skillful midfielders and goal-scoring attackers who often claim the glory, a great team has its foundation in a solid defense. Defenders have to concentrate on doing the ugly—and sometimes painful—things well. They spend their time marking, or guarding, tackling ,and heading the ball and will sometimes come off the field bloodied and bruised.

Defending as a unit

Although there are some great individual defenders, a team also has to work well together to defend effectively. There are two main types of defenders—the center back and the fullback. Teams usually have two of each. The center backs line up close to the goalkeeper, and their job is normally to defend and guard the goal at all costs.

Catenaccio

Catenaccio was a stifling defensive system made famous by an Italian professional team in the 1960s and proved almost impossible to beat. It consisted of five defenders. Four of them shadowed the four opposing strikers, while the fifth was used as a sweeper, staying at the back and sweeping up anything missed by the other defenders. There seemed no way to beat the system until finally a Scottish team unlocked the secret of *catenaccio* and won the 1967 European Cup *(above)*. The Scottish team beat the Italian giants 2–1.

Offside fact

The offside rule was introduced to stop attackers from hanging around their opponents' goal. It can be used by defenders to frustrate strikers who are not allowed to score from an offside position. Players are offside if they are nearer to their opponent's goal line than both the ball and at least two opponents—including the goalkeeper—and are actively involved in the play. A player is not offside if he or she is in his or her own half or is even with or further away from the goal than at least two opponents when the ball is passed. If the player is not involved in the play in any way, the player is also not offside.

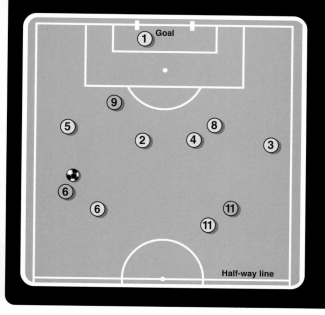

In the example on the left, the last attacker "9" is ahead of the defenders in yellow when "6" plays the ball. As a result, "9" is offside.

Fullbacks, or wingbacks, take a position up wide by the sideline and have a slightly different role. They help out with tackling and marking but will also find space wide on the field so that their teammates can pass to them and an attack can be started. For a defense to work well, the fullbacks have to know exactly when to help out the center backs and when to go wide to help begin an attack.

Roberto Carlos is an attacking fullback for Brazil and Real Madrid. He has won everything from the European Champions League in 1998, 2000, and 2002 to the World Cup with Brazil in 2002.

Last line of defense— the goalkeeper

There is a long running joke in soccer that all goalkeepers are a little crazy. Goalkeeping takes great physical and mental courage, which is probably where the goalie's reputation for craziness comes from. If an field player plays badly, it may not affect the result of the game because his or her teammates can play well to cover up the mistake. But when a goalie makes a mistake, everyone sees it. Of course, saving goals is just as important as scoring them, but goalkeepers are often remembered for their mistakes rather than for the great saves they make.

Top tips for goalkeepers

The great goalkeepers of the past and present—Oliver Kahn of Germany and Carlo Cudicini and Francesco Toldo of Italy—all protect the goal by the same rules. Former international goalkeeping coach Bob Wilson gives these guidelines for goalkeepers:

• expect a shot or a crossing pass at all times

• watch the ball carefully and stay behind the line of its flight

• catch the ball in a relaxed way

• when deflecting the ball, hit it away at an angle

• call loudly to defenders when coming to claim the ball.

Woon Jae Lee of South Korea saves a penalty kick from Joaquim of Spain. Penalty kicks are very difficult to save, and goalkeepers can become heroes when they do prevent a goal.

Tim Howard

Tim Howard is one of the rising stars of international soccer. Following a recent trend of European teams acquiring American goalkeepers, Manchester United, a great English professional team, snapped up the promising Howard from Major League Soccer's (MLS) New York/New Jersey Metrostars in 2003. Howard had won MLS's Goalkeeper of the Year award for two straight years. Sir Alex Ferguson, Manchester United's coach, slated Howard to replace the French World Cup winner Fabien Barthez. Howard's achievement is made all the more impressive because he lives with a serious condition—Tourette's Syndrome, a nervous disorder. Howard, though, has learned to control it and says it does not affect his goalkeeping.

Narrowing the angle fact

An opposing striker is running toward you, and your defenders are nowhere to be seen. Only one thing stands between the onrushing striker and defeat—you, the goalkeeper. These are the key moments of a game, the difference between winning and losing. So how can a goalie swing the odds in his or her favor? Goalkeeping coach Bob Wilson says the keeper should come forward and narrow the angle, thus giving the striker a smaller target at which to aim. The keeper should also try to stay on his or her feet as long as possible, pushing the opponent as wide as possible. Hopefully, the ball will be close enough to block.

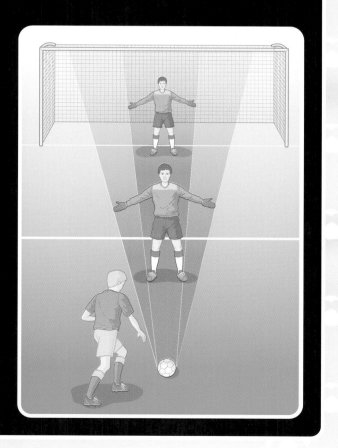

Soccer magic

Nothing excites a soccer crowd more than great skill. The most exciting players are those who light up games with their magic. It is often those magical moments that stay in fans' memories long after the match has ended. Even if a back-heel or bicycle kick does not win a team the game, it can certainly make the price of a ticket worthwhile. These skills are also a great way of surprising opposing defenders.

Giggs on tricks

Ryan Giggs, an English soccer star, is one of the most gifted players of his generation. His range of skills has mesmerized spectators and opposing defenders for more than a decade. The skills are learned in practice, but being able to use them in a game takes talent and instinct.

He says, "All my skills are perfected on the training ground. I don't go into the game having decided to use a particular trick or skill, but if I can do one during the game it gives the crowd and the rest of the team a real lift."

Cruyff turn fact

The Cruyff turn was named after Johan Cruyff, the great Dutch player of the 1970s who first used the skill. When perfected it can leave defenders for dead. The player looks as if he or she is going to pass the ball but instead drags it behind the standing leg with the inside of the foot. He or she then turns into the space left by the defender.

A moment of magic

When Giggs got the ball in the last minute of his league's 1999 semifinal playoff game, there seemed nowhere for him to go. Twenty seconds of magic later, his team had won and was on their way to the championship. Giggs had taken the ball deep inside his own half, run the length of the field, dribbled past six opponents, and smashed the ball into the top corner of the net. The magician had come up with a win from nothing.

Ryan Giggs celebrates after scoring a dramatic goal in a playoff game in 2003. A moment of flair and brilliance can sometimes change a match.

Thierry Henry is a master of the unexpected and the spectacular. Here, the striker attempts to score by using a bicycle kick.

Team play

A team can be full of talented players, but they have to be able to play as a unit. The players must know their jobs, but they must also know how their jobs relate to what the rest of the team is doing. For example, if a player misses a tackle, his or her teammates should be ready to cover the mistake. A team with players of lesser ability can be successful if they stick together and work as a team. Ireland has reached the later stages of three of the last four World Cups, even though they do not have the most talented players. They did this with teamwork and organization.

Team spirit

A team with plenty of spirit has a distinct advantage over a team full of players who do not get along. In order to trust teammates on the field, it is important that players respect each other off of the field. A team full of players wanting to win for each other is much more powerful than one full of players who want to win for themselves. Managers often say good team spirit can be worth an extra ten goals a season.

This team from Scotland is doing their famous pregame huddle. The players link arms to show that they will be playing as a team. This ritual gives each other confidence and makes every player feel like he is an important part of the team.

Germany and the World Cup, 2002

Prior to the 2002 World Cup, some experts described the German team as the worst national team the country had ever produced. They had been soundly beaten 5–1 by England in the qualification rounds. But by playing a disciplined game, playing solid defense, making few mistakes, and sticking together throughout the competition, the Germans went all the way to the championship game where they would play Brazil.

The German coach, Rudi Voller, knew he had less talented players, but he still thought his team had a chance. Before the game he said, "The best team does not always win, otherwise Brazil would have won it fourteen not four times. We know our strengths; we are well-organized, compact, and have great spirit." Germany ended up losing 2–0 but not before proving the value of teamwork.

The South Korea captain, Myung Bo Hong, celebrates scoring the winning penalty against Spain during the quarterfinal of the 2002 World Cup.

Preparing to play —the boss

The role of the coach or manager has changed dramatically over the years. The manager used to just pick the team. Now, the manager or coach is probably the most important person on the club. A modern manager has to be a salesperson, tactician, diplomat, and motivator for the team to be successful. The manager has to select the best personnel, coax the best out of them, and mold all the different personalities into a team. The coach also has to have a sound game plan. And if the team fails to reach its expectations, the manager is the one who pays the price, usually by being fired.

Sven Goran Eriksson

Sven Goran Eriksson is one of the best coaches in the world. He first made his name as manager of a professional team in Sweden before successful jobs coaching in Portugal and Italy. He was a hero in Lazio, the home of an Italian team. He brought them an Italian league title, as well as glory in the European Winner's Cup competition. In 2001, the Swede became England's first foreign manager. He is known for his knowledge of tactics and his ability to motivate players. English star player Michael Owen says, "There are no better managers around in the world. We are very lucky to have him. The players really respect him."

Tactics talk

Before each match, the coach decides on the formation that will best take advantage of the next opponent's weaknesses. Sometimes an attacking formation will be used, and sometimes a defensive one, depending on the opponent. There are three main systems: 4-4-2, 4-3-3, and 3-5-2.

- The 4-4-2 is the most commonly used formation and is neither particularly defensive nor attacking. Here the manager picks four defenders, four midfielders, and two strikers.

- The 4-3-3 is a slightly more attacking system. It still includes four defenders, but there is one less midfielder and one extra attacker. Teams will often switch to this system to give them an extra attacking option.

- The 3-5-2 is the most fluid formation. In other words the system is easily adapted to the state of the game. It includes three central defenders, five midfielders, and two strikers. Of the five midfielders, two stay wide by the sidelines. From there, they can make five defenders or become wingers—to make two extra attackers.

Stress fact

Managing a soccer team at the highest level is so pressure packed that coaches are being warned by doctors to watch their stress levels. In December 2001, Dave Bassett, a coach in the English professional league, was wired up to a heart monitor during a game to test for stress levels. Bassett, then 57 years old, said, "It's a stressful job—but let's face it, lots of jobs are stressful."

The coach has to communicate constantly with the players so the player can carry out precise instructions. Here Real Madrid coach Carlos Queiroz chats with British star David Beckham during a practice.

Food and drink

A soccer player's diet is important to how he or she performs on the field. Eating the right food and drinking the right liquids also greatly affects how quickly a player can recover from an injury. You do not have to go too far back in time to find players preparing for a game with a greasy fried breakfast or a dinner with lots of red meat. With the increase of scientific research, players have now begun to realize the importance of healthy eating and healthy living.

The Wenger diet

When Arsène Wenger of France joined Arsenal, an English professional team, as manager in 1996, he was appalled at the players' eating habits. He knew that the right diet could make his team stronger and less injury-prone than the other English teams. He cut the refined sugar, red meat, fried foods, and fatty dairy products out of the players' diets. He replaced them with vegetables, fish, chicken, and lots of water. He even gave his players urine tests before each morning's practice. This way he could monitor how much water each player was drinking. And it worked, too. In 1998, Arsenal won the English league title and the club championship of Europe.

Heat and humidity

The 2002 World Cup in Japan and South Korea proved a real test for countries unfamiliar with hot climates. Teams from North America and northern Europe were not used to playing in high temperatures and humidity. They had to arrive early to get used to the conditions. If players had been asked to play a game right after stepping off the plane, they would not have been able to perform at anywhere near their best. This is because heat and humidity forces the heart to work harder. The body has to be trained to cope with this. Fitness expert Mark Higginbotham says that it takes two weeks in 79 °F (26 °C) heat—and four when the temperature hits 90 °F (32 °C)—for the human body to get used to these conditions.

Fabio Cannavaro of Italy rehydrates with a drink of water. It is important for players to drink plenty of liquid before, during, and after a game, especially in humid conditions.

Potato power fact

After the 1996 European Championships, French nutritionists criticized the diet of the English team. During the tournament, the English players ate soup, toast, and spaghetti with meat sauce. They should have been eating potatoes. According to nutrition experts, potatoes are ideal for a pregame feast. Potatoes contain glucosides, which offer a steady flow of energy to the muscles. They are also packed with vitamins. Ideally between a half to two-thirds of a pound of boiled potatoes should be eaten about three hours before kickoff.

Conditioning fever

To get to the top in soccer, players have to be in great shape. In order to be ready for the start of a new season, players spend more time working on their conditioning than they do on tactics and ball skills. They have to be in shape enough to play 90-minute games as often as 50 times a season. To reach these levels of fitness, coaches plan routines for their players so that they can build up their strength, speed, and endurance levels. These sessions may not always be a lot of fun, but they are important for team and player preparation.

Members of the English team jog during a training session. Speed and endurance running is a frequent activity so that players can last for the full 90 minutes of a game.

Speed endurance

Training should be similar to a game situation—players need to last for 90 minutes. But soccer is not like long-distance running in which athletes train so that they can pace themselves for a specific length of time. Soccer players have to train their bodies for frequent bursts of speed. To be ready for this, teams spend a lot of time—especially at the start of a season—practicing anaerobic, or speed-endurance training. This involves a slow

Anaerobic training fact

A group of college soccer players designed a program to build up speed endurance. Similar programs are now used all over the world.

Running at about 90 percent speed, players complete 12 runs of 15 yards (13.7 meters) each, followed by 9 runs of 30 yards (27.4 meters), and another 12 runs of 15 yards (13.7 meters). They have a short break—about twenty seconds after each run—with a slightly longer break of two minutes after each set of three. After six weeks, players should be able to complete every run at full speed. They then double their number of mini-runs so they have enough speed endurance to get them through a real game.

Extra time

A team's conditioning is really put to the test when it is reduced to ten players or when a match goes to extra time. This happens in elimination games when the game is still a tie after 90 minutes. England showed great conditioning to last for nearly an hour and a half after David Beckham was ejected in an epic game against Argentina in the 1998 World Cup. Here, Argentinian goalkeeper Carlos Roa saves a penalty kick from England's David Batty. The game went into extra time, finishing 2–2. Argentina won after a series of tiebreaking penalty kicks.

buildup of fitness in preseason, so by the time the first game kicks off, players can last 90 minutes but also remain sharp throughout the game.

Warming up and warming down

Before and after every game or training session, players go through a series of stretching exercises. It is particularly important to stretch calves, groins, and hamstrings, as they can pull or tear quite easily. Stretching gets the body loose and warm before a game and allows it time to recover gradually afterward.

England's Matthew Upson (left) and Wayne Rooney stretch their muscles. This loosens up the body before a game and helps prevent injuries.

Recovering from injury

Today, top professional soccer teams have a full medical staff complete with physiotherapists, nutritionists, and doctors. Soccer is such a big business that teams cannot afford to have their top players sidelined with injuries. Teams will do anything they can to get players back on their feet as soon as possible. Sometimes teams are tempted to field players before they are ready, which can lead to further injuries. As with all things, prevention is better than cure. Scientists and doctors say up to 75 percent of soccer injuries can be prevented if the right precautions are taken.

Ronaldo of Brazil was hurried back into shape so he could play in the 1998 World Cup championship. He was in the hospital just before the game and should not have played. He made his injury worse and for the next three years played very few games.

Here are a few of the simple steps professional soccer players take in order to help them prevent injuries:

- They warm up and cool down.

- They have a sports massage. It helps relieve the lumps and bumps in their bodies, which are what causes muscle tears and strains. A few minutes of massage can also help prevent a potential long-term injury.

- They watch their diet.

- They are in shape. A well-conditioned player is more likely to avoid injury.

- They give themselves enough recovery time. The body needs time to recover from hard exercise. Injuries often occur when a player pushes too hard.

Common injuries and recognizing the signs

The most common soccer injuries are groin strains, pulled hamstrings, knee ligament injuries, sprained ankles, and shin splints. The most serious are broken legs, which can end a player's career. It is important for players to know when they are injured and to do something about it as quickly as possible. Hot spots on the skin, pain, stiffness, swelling, and puffiness are signs that something might be wrong.

Former English star player Stuart Pearce broke his leg during a game. He was given a painkilling spray while still on the field and attempted to play through the pain. He knew the injury was bad but did not realize that his leg was broken.

By continuing to play, Pearce could have done himself serious long-term damage. Luckily he recovered but admitted he had not used his best judgment by trying to stay on the field.

Drugs in soccer

While soccer does not appear to have a major problem with performance-enhancing drugs, there have been a handful of cases in which banned substances have been found in players' blood. Players are given random drug tests in which their urine is tested. If players are found with drugs in their system, they are given a long suspension from the game. Edgar Davids (right) of Holland and Fernando Couto of Portugal are two of the top stars who have been banned for taking illegal drugs.

Emerging champions

The future of soccer around the world looks bright. Soccer in Europe, Latin America, and Africa has always been popular. Many of tomorrow's soccer stars are likely to come from Australia, the United States, and Asia, where the game is growing fast. And as soccer grows, so does the number of exciting young players.

Paving the way

While soccer is producing players of immense talent from all over the world, young U.S. players have been causing the biggest stir recently. Soccer in this country is in a healthy state, with more than three million young people playing in high school and youth organizations. Girls' soccer is also bigger than anywhere else in the world. Women's national teams at U16 (under 16 years old), U17, U19, and U21 levels are securing the future of women's soccer for many years to come, despite the collapse of the Women's United Soccer Association (WUSA) in 2003.

Wondergirl

Lindsay Tarpley *(right)* is a young soccer star destined for the biggest stage. The young forward is already captain of the national U19 team and is a brilliant passer and fantastic goal scorer. Her greatest moment so far was scoring the winning goal against Canada in the final of the first-ever World U19 championships. Tarpley is already knocking on the door of the U.S. national team and was named U.S. Soccer's Young Athlete of the Year in 2002.

Wonderboy

Freddy Adu was just fourteen years old when he signed a contract worth $1 million with Nike. Adu, who plays striker, has scored many goals for every team

for which he has played. At age fourteen, he was already a regular for the U17 national team. He also does not seem to get very nervous playing with people much older than him. In the 2003 Youth World Cup, Adu scored a hat trick! Adu signed a contract with Major League Soccer's (MLS) D.C. United in 2003.

Remember the name

There is no better place to spot future superstars than at the Youth World Cup. In the 2003 U17 tournament in Finland, a few young players lit up the competition enough to suggest they could become the stars of tomorrow. Brazil won the championships with the impressive defender Leonardo. Young Argentinian goalkeeper Oscar Ustari made a string of world-class saves, while one of the leading goal scorers was Colombian striker Carlos Hidalgo. But it was sixteen-year-old Spaniard Francesc "Cesc" Fabregas who stole the show, scoring more goals than anyone else and picking up the best player award.

Sweden's Jane Toernquist (right) stops Germany's Maren Meinert during the 2003 women's World Cup championship game. The United States may be the home of modern women's soccer, but Sweden knocked out the U.S. team in the semifinals. However, it was Germany who went on to win the cup.

The women's game

Although the origins of women's soccer can be found in ancient times, it was not until the early 1900s that the game really took off. By the 1920s, women's soccer was growing in Europe, although most people did not consider it to be a suitable activity for women. When a crowd of 53,000 turned up to watch a women's match in Liverpool, England, it prompted an outrageous reaction from the English Football Association. It issued a statement banning women from playing saying, "[Soccer] is quite unsuitable for ladies." In China, women's soccer was more accepted. In fact it was being taught in schools as early as the 1920s.

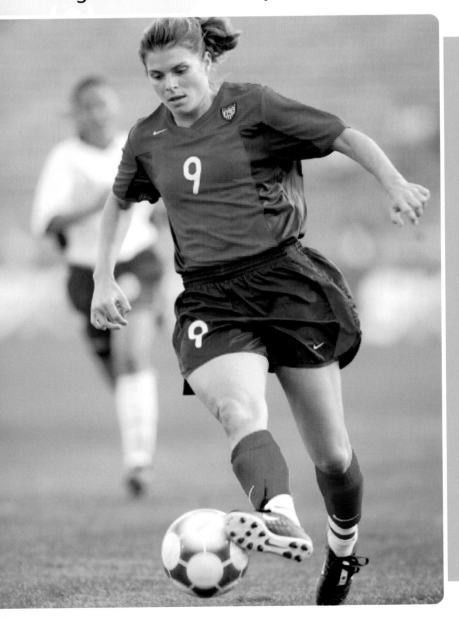

The greatest

One of the finest female soccer players ever to grace the field is forward Mia Hamm. In sixteen years as an international player for the U.S. national team, Hamm had scored a record-shattering 138 goals. She is a supreme dribbler, passer, and finisher and has won medals in the World Cup twice and an Olympic gold once. And how does she do it? "I think the most important thing with soccer is just to have fun with it," she says. And what else? "Practice, practice, practice."

Going professional

In the late 1970s, women's soccer really began to grow. In the beginning, European countries embraced the sport, with Sweden and Germany the most successful. But it was in the United States that women's soccer really exploded. A semi-professional league was set up in the late 1970s. More recently, female players have commanded salaries of up to $85,000 for playing soccer. One women's league folded in 2003, but the Women's Premier Soccer League and W-League continue to grow. Other countries are following the U.S. lead, with the sport beginning to emerge in Nigeria, Australia, and England. A professional women's league was set up in Japan in 1992.

Women's World Cup

The first women's World Cup was played in China in 1991. The U.S. team, nicknamed the Triple-Edged Sword because of the way they tore through the opposition, beat Norway in the final. Although Norway beat Germany in the 1995 tournament, it was the U.S. turn again in 1999. They beat China in front of 90,185 people at the Rose Bowl. The 2003 World Cup was a tournament of upsets, with the U.S. team surprisingly beaten by Sweden in the semifinals. It was Germany who went on to lift the cup, winning all of their matches and scoring 25 goals along the way.

It's all in the head

Soccer is not just about being talented, it is also about being able to handle pressure. When evaluating a player, a coach looks as much at mental toughness as at physical talent. In other words a great player has to be able to play at his or her best in championship matches and championship tournaments. Any talented player can look good in practice, but can he or she play well in an important match in front of thousands of people? Being able to do so separates the good players from the great ones.

The winning mentality

Coaches often talk about the need for their teams to have a winning mentality. This takes confidence, self-belief, and team spirit. If a team falls behind late in a match, it is natural for heads to drop. However, a team with great spirit and confidence will often find a way of getting back into a game—even when it looks impossible.

David Trezeguet

When France beat Italy in the final of the 2000 European Championships, the French were losing 1–0 as the game reached its final minute. However, French substitute Sylvain Wiltord scored a last-gasp equalizer to take the game into overtime. David Trezeguet *(pictured right)* then scored another goal to cap a great win for France. After the game, French coach Roger Lemerre said, "It is true we had our luck, but it was the willpower of the team that won us this trophy."

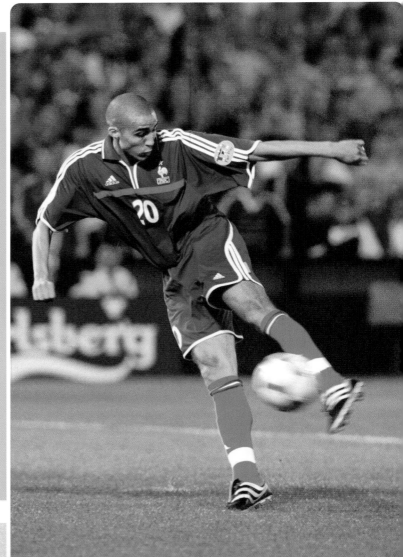

Shoot-out

There is no greater test of a player's nerve than when a game needs a penalty shoot-out to decide its outcome. This happens if a game is tied even after overtime has been played. Five players from each team are chosen to shoot from the penalty spot at the opposing goalkeeper. The team who scores the most penalty kicks wins the match. Without pressure, the odds would be heavily in favor of the kicker. But for players responsible for winning or losing the game, the pressure can sometimes prove too much to bear. Penalty kicks

Results may be important in professional soccer, but sportsmanship should never be forgotten. The International Federation of Football (FIFA) gives out sportsmanship awards to encourage teams to avoid penalties on the field. The award is given to teams with the fewest red and yellow cards. In 2002 the Sportsmanship Award was given to Belgium.

decided the 1994 World Cup final, and it was Italian striker Roberto Baggio who missed the crucial kick. Brazil won and some say Baggio was never the same player again.

Big leagues and continental champs

While there can be no greater thrill for players than to put on their country's national team uniform, professional, or club, teams are usually the livelihood of professional soccer players. Players play for their club team every week, and it is the club that pays the player's salary. Some club competitions—especially in Europe—are almost as important as international tournaments. The Premiership in England, La Liga in Spain, the Bundesliga in Germany, and the Serie A in Italy are considered the most prestigious soccer leagues. However, Major League Soccer (MLS) is rapidly gaining respect in the international soccer world.

Paolo Maldini of AC Milan kisses the the European Champions League trophy after beating another Italian team, Juventus, in 2003.

The Champions League

The European Champions League is the richest team competition in the world. Television networks in Europe pay huge amounts for the right to show the games. The league brings together the best club teams in Europe such as Italy's AC Milan, Germany's Bayern Munich, and Spain's Real Madrid. The teams are split into groups with the top teams from each group advancing to the quarterfinals. The winners take home the European Cup.

Preparing for major championships

The World Cup is only played every four years. There are other championships that are held on each continent. Some of the major ones include the European Championship, the African Nations Cup, and Copa America, the championship of the Americas.

Major League Soccer

Before it hosted the 1994 World Cup, the United States promised to form a professional soccer league. By 1996 MLS was up and running. The league is growing in popularity and gets bigger and better with every season. The 2003 MLS Cup was played in front of a capacity crowd of 27,000 fans at the Home Depot Center in Carson, California. The San Jose Earthquake beat the Chicago Fire 4–2, and professional soccer seems to have taken root. The league is now attracting good players from Europe and South America and with crowds and television revenue up, the future looks bright for MLS.

In a major championship, countries are divided into four- or five-team groups. Then the top one or two teams from that group advance to the quarterfinals. Prior to the tournament, the teams play a series of practice matches so the coaches can decide which players to take to the tournament. The coach should make sure these games are played in similar conditions to those the team will face in the championship. A coach will usually have the whole squad (around 22 players) together for four weeks before a tournament to build up team spirit and to work on team play.

Hatem Trabelsi of Tunisia is taken down by Noureddine Naybet of Morocco in the 2004 African Nations Cup. Tunisia won the championship in front of their own fans.

Crowning of a champ— the World Cup

Every soccer player dreams of playing in a World Cup. It is what makes the endless hours of training and the cold midwinter matches worthwhile. It is also an opportunity to become a household name around the world.

History

The World Cup has become bigger each time it is played. The first World Cup in 1930 was won by the South American hosts Uruguay. Since then, when just thirteen teams competed for the trophy, the game has exploded in popularity. In the 2002 World Cup, 32 teams battled for the game's biggest prize. As with every tournament before it, reputations were made and championship memories were formed by the time the trophy was awarded.

The 1970 World Cup

The Brazilian team that beat Italy in the memorable 1970 World Cup final in Mexico is thought by many to be the greatest team ever to have played the game.
Packed with flair and skill, it was also better prepared than other teams—working together as a unit and stifling team after team in the process. In the championship, the Brazilians had four of the best players in the world—Carlos Alberto, Jairzinho, Rivelino, and Pelé *(center)*. The free-flowing Brazilians overcame heat, altitude, and the excellent defense of the Italians to win 4–1.

The biggest stage of all

A few good performances in a World Cup can make a player or coach world famous, but reputations can also be ruined by the tournament. Every player wants to be at the top of his or her game when the World Cup comes around. El Hadji Diouf of Senegal dazzled the world in 2002, and Oliver Kahn was even better. The German goalkeeper won the Golden Ball award for best player in the competition. In addition, current MLS players Landon Donovan of the San Jose Earthquake and DaMarcus Beasley of the Chicago Fire established themselves as world-class players when they helped lead the United States to the quarterfinals in the 2002 World Cup.

Senegal player El Hadji Diouf made his name with a great performance against the previous World Cup champion France in 2002.

Into the future

Soccer is a truly global game. It is a way of life for thousands of people. The game offers an opportunity for talented players from the poorest parts of the world to become the soccer champs of tomorrow. Now, individuals and corporate sponsors continue to support soccer throughout the world. This support should ensure the future of the game, allowing it to thrive and grow for years to come.

African soccer

The great Brazilian player Pelé predicted that an African team would win the World Cup before the end of the 1900s. Although that did not happen, there is no doubt the prediction will come true sooner rather than later. Cameroon was the first to make the soccer world take notice when it reached the quarterfinals of the 1990 World Cup. Since then Nigeria, South Africa, and Senegal have also burst onto the world scene.

The new world

Nowhere is soccer growing faster than in the United States. In 2004 the U.S. national team was ranked in the top ten in the world soccer rankings. Even though the best U.S. players still play in Europe, Major League Soccer's (MLS) improved facilities and competition are making many think twice before going overseas. In addition to Crew Stadium in Columbus, Ohio, and the Home Depot Center in Carson, California, the New York/New Jersey Metrostars are building a new stadium in Harrison, New Jersey, that is scheduled to open in 2006. In 2003,

Forty-year-old Roger Milla (right) dazzles spectators at the 1990 World Cup. African soccer had arrived.

the 10-team league drew more than 2 million fans in 150 games. On July 4, 2003, more than 60,000 fans came out to see Kansas City play a pivotal game at Colorado. In addition, Landon Donovan, DaMarcus Beasley, and Freddy Adu will keep fans coming out to watch MLS games for years to come.

Down under

Australian soccer is growing fast. It boasts world-class players such as Mark Viduka, Brett Emerton, and Harry Kewell and has recently beaten top competition, including England. For the game to succeed, though, Australia must qualify for the World Cup. They have qualified only once in their history.

Brett Emerton of Australia, who plays professionally in England, scored Australia's third goal in its exhibition against England in 2003.

The Columbus Crew and Chicago Fire battle it out in a match in 2003. Here, defender Nelson Akwari (left) of Columbus steals the ball from Chicago forward Nate Jaqua.

The modern soccer star

Being a world-class soccer player today is hard work but rewarding. Those who get to the top can be richly rewarded, but it is a short career. Most professionals are able to play at a high level for about fifteen years if they are lucky. The world's best soccer players are like pop stars—rich and famous. But soccer is also physically demanding. Players work hard and train for long hours and can be away from home for long stretches at a time.

English soccer player David Beckham stands with his wife Victoria. He proudly displays an award he received from Queen Elizabeth II at Buckingham Palace on November 27, 2003.

Always on the move

Most professional players move teams several times in a career, often to teams in another country. They do this for many reasons. Sometimes teams cannot afford to keep a player, and sometimes players want to move to bigger clubs. International players also spend a lot of time with their national teams—especially when a major championship is being played.

Win some, lose some

Soccer stars can win the adoration of thousands one day and bear the brunt of the anger of the next. English midfielder David Beckham is probably the most famous soccer player in the world. Today, he is admired by millions. After the 1998 World Cup, however, things were very different. English fans blamed Beckham when their country was knocked out of the World Cup. Beckham was given a red card after a foul and ejected from

George Weah (above) of Liberia and AC Milan understood what it meant to give something back to the game. Weah paid for his country's trip to the African Nations Cup.

crucial match against Argentina. The press and public treated him unfairly. Hardly a day went by when the newspapers did not carry a story about his private life. The pressures of his lifestyle would have been unbearable to most people. But after working hard on and off the field, he is now one of the best loved celebrities in Great Britain. Three years after Beckham's ejection, he scored a last-minute goal that secured England's qualification to the 2002 World Cup.

An athlete's world, though, is full of ups and downs. In the quarterfinals of the 2004 European Championships, Beckham missed a penalty shot against Portugal that ended up costing England the game.

Giving something back

It may be hard work, but professional soccer players consider themselves lucky. They are paid for doing something they love. Most players try to give something back to the community—perhaps by visiting hospitals or donating money to causes they support. Liberian player George Weah, one of the world's best players in the 1990s, was also a very generous person. He discovered his country did not have enough money to pay for Liberia's national team to travel to the African Nations Cup. So, he paid all their expenses himself.

Soccer records

Soccer players are no different from other athletes. They strive to be the best, and they like to break records. Fans like records, too. They fuel the passion and pride that fans have for their clubs and countries. Below is a selection of records illustrating some of the game's highest achievers. There is also a listing of a few key dates in the game's history.

World Cup Winners	
Team	Number of times won
Brazil	5
Italy	3
Germany	3
Uruguay	3
Argentina	2
England	1
France	1

Most World Cup Career Goals	
Player/Country	Goals
Gerd Muller, West Germany	14
Just Fontaine, France	13
Pelé, Brazil	12
Ronaldo, Brazil	12

Recent World [Soccer Player] of the Year			
Year	Player	Club	Country
2003	Zinedine Zidane	Real Madrid	France
2002	Ronaldo	Real Madrid	Brazil
2001	Luis Figo	Real Madrid	Portugal

Key Dates in Soccer	
Year	Event
1862	Notts County becomes the world's first professional club
1863	English Football Association is formed
1874	Shin guards are introduced to protect players' legs
1875	Crossbar is introduced in place of the tape, which used to run between each post
1925	Offside rule is introduced
1930	First World Cup is won by Uruguay; United States reaches the semifinals
1991	United States wins the first women's World Cup

Amazing World Records fact

Pelé scored more professional goals than anyone in history. The Brazilian scored a staggering 1,281 goals in his career. He broke every scoring record in his country before becoming the only player to win three World Cups. In international matches, he scored an average of one goal per game.

World Cup Records

Record	Result/Holders
Largest World Cup winning margin	10–1, Hungary over El Salvador, 1982
Most World Cup appearances	25, Lothar Mattaus, Germany
Most goals in a World Cup	13, Just Fontaine, France, 1958
Most goals in a World Cup match	5, Oleg Salenko of Russia vs. Cameroon, 1994

World Soccer Records

Record	Result/Holders
Largest international winning margin	31–0, Australia vs. American Samoa, 2001
Biggest crowd for a soccer game	199,854, Brazil vs. Uruguay, Maracana Stadium, Brazil, 1930 World Cup final
World's highest-paid player	$84 million, Zinedine Zidane, 2001
Most appearances on a national team	160, Hossam Hassan, Egypt, 1985–2002

U.S. Soccer Records

Men's National Team	Result/Holders
Biggest margin in international win	7–0, vs. El Salvador, 1993
Most international appearances	154, Cobi Jones
Most international goals	34, Eric Wynalda
World Cup—Year, Location	**Result**
1930, Uruguay	Semifinals, lost 6–1 to Argentina
1934, Italy	First round, lost 7–1 to Italy
1950, Brazil	Lost in group stage
1990, West Germany	Lost in group stage
1994, United States	Round of 16, lost 1–0 to Brazil
1998, France	Lost in group stage
2002, Japan and South Korea	Quarterfinals, lost 1–0 to Germany
Women's World Cup—Year, Location	**Result**
1991, China	Champions, beat Norway 2–1 in finals
1995, Sweden	Semifinals, lost 1–0 to Norway
1999, United States	Champions, beat China 5–4 in finals
2003, United States	Semifinals, lost 3–0 to Germany
MLS Champions, 1997–2003	**Most Valuable Player**
1997, D.C. United	Jaime Moreno
1998, Chicago Fire	Peter Nowak
1999, D.C. United	Ben Olsen
2000, Kansas City Wizards	Tony Meola
2001, San Jose Earthquake	Dwayne DeRosario
2002, Los Angeles Galaxy	Carlos Ruiz
2003, San Jose Earthquake	Landon Donovan

Statistics in this book were correct at time of going to press.

Glossary

back-heel move using a heel to pass the ball backwards

bicycle kick overhead-kick. A player with his or her back to goal hooks the ball over his or her shoulder to try to score.

extra time time added at the end of an elimination match so the outcome of the game can be decided

foul deliberate or accidental infringement of the rules of a sport or game

free-flowing the passage of play involving quick passing and keeping possession of the ball

free kick call by the referee after a player is fouled. The opposition has to be at least eleven yards (ten meters) away from the kicker, leaving him or her free to aim the ball in the direction she or he chooses.

give and go quick passing move between two players. One passes the ball, and the other returns the pass.

hat trick occurs when a player scores three goals in a game

marking when a defensive player guards, or marks, an opposing attacker to stop him or her from scoring

penalty when a player is fouled inside the penalty box, a referee gives the fouled player's side a kick at goal. Only the shooter and the opposing goalkeeper are allowed in the box while the kick is being taken. The kick is taken from the penalty spot, thirteen yards (twelve meters) away from the goal.

sidelined hurt or not well enough to play for the team

substitute reserve player. Teams are allowed a number of reserves (either three or five) who can come on to the field in place of one of the players who started the game. Substitutes can be used for tactical reasons or because a player is injured.

tackle move by a defending player to take the ball away from his or her opponent. The defending player slides in from the side with his or her foot first and knocks the ball away from his or her opponent. It is a foul if the defender slides in from behind or if he or she trips the offensive player without hitting the ball.

Resources

Major international and U.S. organizations

AYSO-American Youth Soccer Organization
National Support and Training Center
12501 S. Isis Avenue
Hawthorne, Calif. 90250
800-872-2976

MLS-Major League Soccer
110 E. 42nd Street, 10th Floor
New York, N.Y. 10017
212-450-1200

WUSA-Women's United Soccer Association
6205 Peachtree Dunwoody Road, 15th Floor
Atlanta, Ga. 30328
404-269-8800

U.S. Soccer Federation,
1801 S. Prairie Avenue
Chicago, Ill. 60616
312-808-1300

MISL-Major Indoor Soccer League
1175 Post Road East
Westport, Conn. 06880
203-222-4900

FIFA-International Football Association
FIFA House, Hitziweg House 11,
PO Box 85, 8030
Zurich, Switzerland

Further reading

Collie, Ashley Jude. *World of Soccer: A Complete Guide to the World's Most Popular Sport*. New York City: Rosen Publishing Group, 2003.

Cope, Suzanne. *Great Soccer: Team Offense*. Danbury, Conn.: Scholastic Library Publishing, 2001.

Layden, Joe. *Superstars of U.S.A. Women's Soccer 2000*. New York City: Simon and Schuster Children's Publishing, 2000.

Rutledge, Rachel. *The Best of the Best in Soccer*. Brookfield, Conn.: Millbrook, 2000.

Index